Chris Bonington's
LAKELAND HERITAGE

CHRIS BONINGTON
WITH
ROLY SMITH

HALSGROVE

First published in Great Britain in 2004

British Library Cataloguing-in-Publication Data
A CIP record for this title is available from the British Library

ISBN 1 84114 395 2

HALSGROVE
Halsgrove House
Lower Moor Way
Tiverton, Devon EX16 6SS
Tel: 01884 243242
Fax: 01884 243325
email: sales@halsgrove.com
website: www.halsgrove.com

Printed and bound by CPI Bath Press, Bath.

CONTENTS

Foreword by Sir Chris Bonington, CBE   5

Ken Portway (1922–2004)   7

One **The Southern Lakes**   8

Two **The Northern Lakes**   23

Three **The Dales**   49

Four **The Peaks**   67

Five **The Passes**   81

Six **The Tarns**   95

Seven **Waterfalls**   99

Eight **Towns and Villages**   105

Nine **Churches and Castles**   127

Ten **Buildings and Monuments**   137

Eleven **Youth Hostels**   149

Twelve **Literary Landmarks**   153

Sir Chris Bonington, CBE.

LAKELAND HERITAGE

Foreword by Sir Chris Bonington, CBE

I've always loved old pictures of places I know well or perhaps am just visiting, be they on the walls of people's homes, in their albums or in books. Ones of the Lake District are extra special to me since it is my adopted home, and a place I have come to love more than anywhere else on Earth. It is always a delight to see a photograph or picture of a familiar scene as it was fifty or a hundred years ago, to recognise buildings and the eternal shapes of fell and lake.

So it was a special and welcome surprise to receive a hand-written letter in August 2003 from Ken Portway. He had kindly written to me on three previous occasions to congratulate me on my climbs, and now he was offering to give me his collection of postcards of the Lake District, some of which dated back over a hundred years. He was a keen fell walker with a deep love of the Lakes.

I was immensely touched and even more delighted when the parcel containing the postcards arrived at home some weeks later. They were a wonderful, nostalgic treasure trove – something that I felt I had to share with others rather then just keep for myself. I therefore hit on the idea of trying to find a publisher and to donate the proceeds of the book to a worthwhile charity.

I contacted an old friend, Roly Smith, editorial manager of Halsgrove Publishing, who was enthusiastic about the idea and has written the captions for the postcards. We agreed that royalties from the book should go to the Council for National Parks, the charity of which I had been president for eight years and which has done a wonderful job to help maintain the beauty and health of our National Parks including, of course, the Lake District.

Sadly, once we had got this project underway and I wrote to Ken to get his approval, I learnt from his brother, Hugh Archbold, that Ken had died on 1 April, 2004 from a heart attack. This book is therefore dedicated to him.

DEDICATION
TO KEN PORTWAY

Ken Portway stands by the summit cairn on Dale Head
in the north western fells of his beloved Lake District.

KEN PORTWAY
(1922–2004)

Ken Portway of West Denton, Newcastle-upon-Tyne, who died after a heart attack at the age of eighty-two on 1 April, 2004, was an ardent lover of the Lake District and an avid postcard collector.

According to Agnes, his wife of fifty-five years, he obtained most of his cards from local flea markets, and was always on the lookout to add to his considerable collection.

'The Lake District was always top of his list,' explained Agnes in her warm Geordie accent. 'We had some fantastic times ourselves on holiday in the Lakes, staying at places like Keswick. Although I always loved Borrowdale and I remember us climbing Helm Crag once, I don't think Ken had a particularly favourite place – he just loved it all.'

Ken had worked in the Housing Department at Newcastle City Council for twenty-eight years before his retirement. Born and bred like Agnes in Newcastle, he had enlisted in the Royal Artillery for seven years during the Second World War, serving in North Africa and Italy. The couple were both stalwarts of the United Reformed Church near their home in West Denton for forty years, and they had no children.

'We travelled the world with his postcards,' recalled Agnes. 'Whenever a friend or relative went abroad for a holiday, he always asked them to send him a postcard. Then out would come his *Times* atlas, and we'd trace wherever they were in the world and the postcard would go into the collection. I remember once someone did a tour across America, and we were sent a card from every state – about 20 in all.

'I know that Ken would be delighted to know that his postcard collection, and his memory, was being celebrated in this way – especially as he wanted them to go to one of his heroes, Chris Bonington, with whom he corresponded regularly.

'He was a lovely man and is sadly missed.'

This 1904 coloured postcard gives a romantic, almost unrecognisable, view of Waterhead, Windermere, making it look more like Switzerland than Westmorland.

ONE

THE SOUTHERN LAKES

Pinafore-clad waitresses serve suited customers on the lawns of the 'Old England Hotel' on the shores of Windermere – England's largest lake – in this Abraham photograph which seems to have been taken in the 1920s.

This hand-coloured postcard is entitled 'Windermere – a peep at the ferry' and shows the site of the original hand-rowed ferry service across the narrowest part of Windermere at Bowness Nab. In the background are the wooded Claife Heights on the western side of the lake.

A mid-Fifties view of Bowness on Windermere, showing the various steamers and pleasure craft which allowed visitors to explore the lake. The message on the back of this postcard is amusing: 'By gum, I nearly got tippy here'.

The two postcards, left and below, show what could be done with a little of what today would be called 'manipulation' by the photographer – in this case George Abraham of Keswick. The first one is labelled 'an actual photograph' and shows Shorthorn cattle drinking in the lake at Winderwere near Ferry Nab on an August afternoon.

The second shows virtually the same shot, but this time it has been heavily romanticised with the insertion of a lowering sun (or moon?) illuminating the waters of the lake.

Jenkin's (or Jenkyn's) Crag is a famous viewpoint at the northern end of Windermere, hidden in the trees of Dovenest Wood above Wansfell Holme. We are looking south down the lake here, towards wooded Latterbarrow on the right with Belle Isle blocking the lake in the far distance.

Windermere & Langdale Pikes.

The distinctive profile of the Langdale Pikes, as seen across Windermere from above Low Wood on the eastern shore in this hand-coloured, 1903 postcard.

ELTERWATER AND LANGDALE PIKES

Snow was dusting the tops of the Langdale Pikes in the right distance when this photograph was taken across Elterwater, the small lake which fills the lower end of the Langdale valley near Skelwith Bridge.

It's bluebell time on the slopes above Rydal Water in this postcard from 1959. Rydal Water is the small lake on the River Rothay between Windermere and Grasmere.

'Dora's Field' on the slopes above Rydal Water is named after William Wordsworth's favourite child. The family, which included his wife, Mary, his sister Dorothy and his three surviving children, lived nearby at Rydal Mount between 1813 until the poet's death in 1850.

Another view of Rydal Water with some obliging sheep, including local Herdwicks, providing the foreground. William Wordsworth kept himself fit, and was a keen skater on the lake when it froze in winter. In 1830, Dorothy wrote: 'He is still the crack skater on Rydal Lake, and, as to climbing of mountains, the hardiest and the youngest are yet hardly a match for him.'

White Moss Common, between Rydal Water and Grasmere, is now a nature reserve and an important surviving wetland for wildlife. This 1960s view looks east and shows Rydal Water from the nobbly height of White Moss itself.

Above and right: Nab Scar is the prominent crag above Nab Cottage, a former home of both De Quincey and Coleridge, on the northern shore of Rydal Water. This pair of scenes taken from almost identical spot, shows the crag in profile looking west towards the central Lakeland hills. The second shot is another of Abraham's 'real photographs' from a postcard of the 1960s.

A rather heavily hand-coloured postcard which incorrectly describes this as 'Grasmere lake' when in fact it is Rydal Water with Nab Scar beyond. The rowing boat in the left foreground invitingly awaits.

The rough slopes of Loughrigg dominate the southern shores of Rydal Water, and Loughrigg Terrace, the path which runs diagonally across its slopes, is a well-known excursion with splendid views across both Grasmere and Rydal Water.

RYDAL WATER AND WANSFELL.

This view looks south east across the calm surface of Rydal Water towards the serrated skyline of Wansfell, the mountain which overlooks Ambleside in the valley below.

A glimpse of the northern end of Grasmere, with Helm Crag prominent to the right, from Wishing Gate on the climb to White Moss above the eastern shore of the lake.

Wishing Gate is the name of the minor road which winds up the slopes of White Moss from the eastern shores of Grasmere. We are looking across the lake to Silver Howe, and the charming message on this 1902 postcard says: 'I am sending you a wishing gate, so wish something very nice to happen to you.'

WISHING GATE, GRASMERE.

The ubiquitous Shorthorn cattle are enjoying a cool dip in Grasmere, with the heights of Silver Howe beyond, in this 1908 postcard. The writer said she was enjoying her holiday, but going 'rather slow.'

Another view of Grasmere from almost the same spot, this time looking a little further north towards Wray Gill on Silver Howe.

Fir Crag, on the western shore of Grasmere, is well-named in this Abraham photograph, which looks across to the village of Grasmere with the Fairfield range in the background.

Looking towards Helm Crag in the distance from a boat as it rounds the rocky shores of the unnamed island in the middle of Grasmere.

628. GRASMERE FROM RED BANK.
(ABRAHAM'S SERIES.)

Another view of Grasmere's island, this time looking down on it and the village from Red Bank Wood above Dale End, towards the distant pass of Dunmail Raise, with Fairfield to the right.

"GRASMERE'S PEACEFUL VALE"
122. GRASMERE LAKE AND VILLAGE.

Above and below: Two views of Grasmere from Hunting Stile above the western shore, looking towards Heron Pike, the peak in the right centre, with Fairfield on the left. The Abraham caption titles the first photograph 'Grasmere's peaceful vale', while the second, hand-coloured postcard is from a slightly higher viewpoint and dates from 1913.

379. *Haweswater from Measand.*

Haweswater is an artificially-expanded lake formed by the damming of the Mardale Beck and the drowning of Mardale village in the 1930s. This view is taken from Measland End, an outlier of High Raise on the northern shores of the lake, looking south.

4016. HAYESWATER and HIGH STREET.

Lowe, Patterdale
Copyright.

Deep in the heart of the hills, Hayeswater lies below the Straights of Riggendale and the long ridge of High Street, between Mardale and Hartsop. This is an area where today, if you are lucky, you might just spot one of the Lake District's rarest birds – a golden eagle.

This is perhaps the most famous view in the whole Lake District, so instantly-recognisable that it was adopted by the Lake District National Park for its logo. It shows Yewbarrow (left), Great Gable (centre) and Lingmell (right) standing in perfect symmetry around the head of Wast Water.

Another stormy version of the same view, this time dating from 1911 and showing a little more of the upper slopes of Lingmell to the left, which lead up to England's highest mountain of Scafell Pike.

Perhaps the most famous geological feature of Wast Water are the Screes, a mile-long curtain of constantly shifting rock debris which spills down straight into the lake from the slopes of Illgill Head above.

TWO

THE NORTHERN LAKES

The present Thirlmere was created in 1879 as a reservoir to provide the fast-expanding city of Manchester with water. It drowned two existing lakes called Leatheswater and Brackmere, which had a footbridge across their middle. This view from 1909 shows the newly-constructed dam at the northern end of the lake.

THIRLMERE AND HELVELLYN.

A.441

A romantic water-colourist's view of Thirlmere with Helvellyn rising on its eastern shore. The minor road which winds along the western shore has conveniently been excluded.

"THE HOME OF THE BREEZES"
142 THIRLMERE AND HELVELLYN.

A photographic version of the same view, looking south down the lake from near Raven Crag. It is romantically-titled 'The home of the breezes.'

RAVEN CRAG, THIRLMERE.

Raven Crag is the most impressive rocky outcrop on the western shores of Thirlmere, and is a favourite haunt of rock climbers. The picture has more than an echo of the images of the head of Buttermere, with the pines stepping out into the lake and Shorthorn cattle enjoying a peaceful drink.

THIRLMERE.

This is a another imaginative, turn of the last century, painter's view of Thirlmere, looking more like the North West Highlands of Scotland than the Lake District. Raven Crag is on the right, with Helvellyn giving more than a passing impression of Ben Nevis!

We are looking north down Thirlmere in this 1907 postcard, which shows Blencathra (or Saddleback) in the background and the wooded hump of Great How in the right middle distance. The correspondent had walked the 15 miles from Ambleside to Kendal the day before.

The opposite end of the lake, looking north from above the white painted farm house of Steel End, soon after the reservoir's construction. Today, serried ranks of conifers cloak the sides of the lake, planted by the water company in the interests of water purity.

BOAT LANDING, DERWENTWATER

The peak of Causey Pike is reflected in the waters of Derwent Water in this heavily-enhanced photograph of the boat landing at Waterhead, near Keswick. Note the sailing boat on the right and the lone oarsman, centre.

One of the most famous and photographed scenes in the whole district is pine-topped Friar's Crag, on the eastern shores of Derwent Water, close to Keswick. It is seen here in this Abraham photograph with a snow-covered Grisedale Pike rising across the lake.

A wider-angle view of the same scene, with Causey Pike now taking prominence across the lake. This is another Abraham brothers photograph, entitled 'An autumn morning.'

Night has fallen, and a 'hunter's moon' rides through the clouds above Causey Pike, its silvery rays reflected in the surface of the lake.

This is Friar's Crag seen from the opposite direction, looking towards the long escarpment of rocks known as Walla Crags, on the eastern shores of Derwent Water.

There are four islands on Derwent Water, and this one shows wooded Derwent Isle from Friar's Crag, with a family of foxes conveniently posing in the foreground.

One of the best views of Derwent Water and the surrounding fells can be seen from the short climb up to Castle Head, near Keswick. Here we can see, right to left, St Herbert's Island, Lord's Island and Rampsholme Island, with the slopes of Maiden Moor and High Spy in the background, leading the eye into Borrowdale.

Probably the most popular viewpoint in the whole of the Lake District, and certainly one of the most photographed, Ashness Bridge is where the narrow road leading up from Barrow Bay, Derwent Water to the picturesque hamlet of Watendlath crosses the Watendlath Beck. Derwent Water is backed by the smooth slopes of Siddaw in the misty background.

Seen from above Barrow Bay, Derwent Water. Barrow House, the large house in the left centre, is now the 88-bed Derwent Water Youth Hostel. The view looks south into the 'Jaws of Borrowdale.'

'Waterlily Bay' Derwent Water, is not marked on any maps, but seems to have existed, with its resident pair of mute swans, somewhere near the landing stage at Mary Mount, near the Lodore Hotel.

A similar viewpoint with a boatman resting among the water lilies, but this time we can see the mock-Gothic towers of the Lodore Hotel in the distance, beneath Shepherd's Crag with a glimpse of Lodore Falls.

Catbells is a beautiful and easily-attained little hill (1482ft) which is a favourite first ascent for children of hill-walking families. And it has the reward of one of the finest views in Lakeland, northwards down the expanse of Derwent Water towards the distant slopes of Skiddaw.

2106. DERWENTWATER FROM SKIDDAW HUT.

Skiddaw Hut was a convenient refreshment point for climbers about half-way up the long plod of the ascent of 3054ft Skiddaw from Keswick. Now long gone, the site nevertheless provides a superb view southwards, with the expanse of Derwent Water spread out like a map below.

Those two swans make another appearance in this heavily-romanticised painting of Derwent Water by F.W.Hayes from 1903. The message to a correspondent in Newcastle-upon-Tyne, sarcastically states: 'This is <u>not</u> the lake at the top of the Dene.'

An Abraham view from high in the fells above the Honister Pass shows the twin lakes of the Buttermere Valley – Buttermere and Crummock Water – to good effect. They were once one lake, split into two by alluvium from the Sail Beck and Sour Milk Gill.

The minor road to Buttermere from Lorton Vale winds along the lake's eastern shore, with a ring of fells at its head, from Honister Crag (left) to Haystacks on the right.

A closer, watercolourist's view of the head of Buttermere, again showing Honister Crag and Fleetwith Pike and a cloud-cloaked Haystacks.

The famous string of Scots pines leading out into Buttermere can be seen in the middle distance of this view of the head of the lake from Hassness.

Another of Lakeland's most famous viewpoints. This is a hand-coloured photographic postcard of the head of Buttermere, with the bulk of High Crag forming the backdrop.

Buttermere's twin Crummock Water has a more open, rocky aspect than its neighbour. This view, entitled 'Solitude', shows Mellbreak (left) and Red Pike in the background.

A painted version of 'Solitude', the same scene as the previous postcard, with the rowing boat replaced by a lonely heron. The rocky outcrop on the left is correctly identified as Rannerdale Knotts but Red Pike is wrongly described as Whiteless Pike, which is near Grasmoor.

MELLBRAKE, SHOWING CRUMMOCKWATER AND BUTTERMERE IN THE DISTANCE.

Looking south down Buttermere from Low Fell towards Crummock Water and just a glimpse of Buttermere. Mellbreak is the prominent fell on the right.

4033. Loweswater and Melbreak.

Little-visited Loweswater, the third lake in the Buttermere system, may not have the dramatic mountain scenery of the other two, but lowly Mellbreak, seen here in the centre, makes a good show. Shorthorns graze in the pastoral foreground.

Ullswater, 7½ miles long and in three quite distinct reaches, is many peoples' favourite lake and this is reflected by the number of postcards of it in Ken Portway's collection. This 1934 postcard view looks down on Howtown Bay on the southern shore from the slopes of Swarth Fell.

Seen from the other side of the lake, Hallin Fell assumes a really mountainous aspect, overlooking the sheltered bay of Howtown, the popular destination of lake cruises from Glenridding.

The head of Ullswater, looking towards Patterdale with Arniston Crag peeping above the conifers on the right.

A coach-and-four conveniently stops for one of the Abraham brothers to take a photograph looking south near Gowbarrow Park on the northern shores of Ullswater.

The ubiquitous Shorthorn cattle were once the most common beef and dairy breed in northern England, as this 'Cattle Scene' by the Abraham brothers shows. In the background is Glenridding and the head of Ullswater.

After a rain storm, sunlight bursts through the clouds in 'Jacob's Ladders' of light, reflected in the calm waters of Ullswater with Place Fell rising across the lake on the left.

Looking down on the little hamlet of Glenridding at the southern end of Ullswater, with Birk Fell rising across the water. The message on the back of the postcard states: 'This place is T.H.(top hole?). A stream runs right in front of the house, so I will be able to fish from my bed.'

Ullswater and Glenridding from the foot of Place Fell, looking west towards Helvellyn.

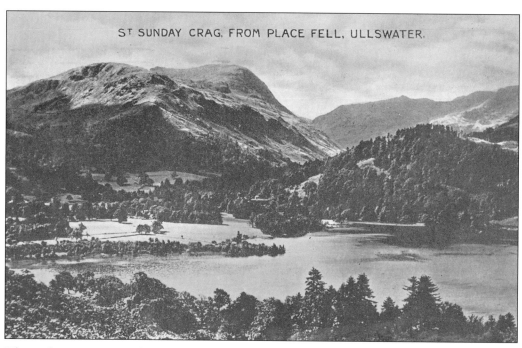

The rocky escarpment of St Sunday Crag is a northern outlying ridge from Fairfield, seen here looking across Ullswater from the slopes of Place Fell.

Another view of St Sunday Crag in the distance looking across the lake to the wooded height of Keldas and into Patterdale.

Looking south where the Goldrill Beck enters Ullswater at Patterdale, with Caudale Moor rising in the background.

In some views such as this one St Sunday Crag dominates the head of Ullswater. Again cattle have been used to create a pastoral foreground to the 'Oilette' postcard.

Another 'Oilette' postcard with a strategically-placed boatman, showing the scene from Glencoyne, looking across the lake to Birk Fell with Place Fell beyond.

Described as 'Ullswater from the Coach Road', this Abraham's photograph is taken from a similar viewpoint to that at the bottom of p.39, where a coach is actually shown.

Stybarrow Bay is on the south-western shore of Ullswater, just north of Glenridding. Here we are looking south across the lake towards Glenridding.

380 STYBARROW CRAG, ULLSWATER.
(ABRAHAMS' SERIES)

Wooded Stybarrow Crag drops vertically into the waters of Ullswater, so can be explored by boat, as these two visitors were doing on this postcard which dates from 1913.

Ullswater from Gowbarrow Park Brow, looking north towards the encircling fells of the Fairfield and Helvellyn ranges.

The Raven at Pooley Bridge, Ullswater   S.644

The Raven was a steam–powered pleasure boat which took passengers for cruises the length of Ullswater, from Glenridding in the south to Pooley Bridge at its northernmost extremity, where it is seen moored.

William Wordsworth's poem *Daffodils* is probably the best-remembered in the English language. It was the result of a walk he took in April, 1802 with his beloved sister Dorothy along the shores of Ullswater, where according to Dorothy's *Journals:*

> *I never saw daffodils so beautiful they grew among the mossy stones about and about them, some rested their heads upon these stones as on a pillow for weariness and the rest tossed and reeled and danced and seemed as if they verily laughed with the wind that blew upon them over the lake...*

It is interesting to compare that description with the famous poem.

The only true 'lake' in the Lake District, Bassenthwaite Lake lies to the north of Keswick and Derwent Water. This unusual view from the western side of the lake shows the summit of Skiddaw on the left, with the crags of Ullock Pike in the centre.

THREE

THE DALES

A famous view of the Langdale Pikes, with Harrison Stickle the highest summit seen on the right, Pike How and Pike of Stickle in the centre, and Raven Crag to the left of Pike How. The Dungeon Ghyll Hotel can be seen in the centre.

This is an almost exact painted version of the previous postcard, with the Dungeon Ghyll shrunken to almost non-existence and the peaks sharpened by the exercise of artistic licence.

The same view in a hand-coloured, 1908 postcard, with the famous white-walled climbers' base of the Dungeon Ghyll Hotel just over the bridge, and a pony and trap parked on the extreme right.

LANGDALE PIKES.

A closer view of the Dungeon Ghyll Hotel in a 1906 postcard. Behind the hotel, which was one of the birth-places of British rock climbing, the slopes of Pike How and Harrison Stickle beckon the climber.

Another cradle of rock climbing was Wasdale, and this coloured Abraham postcard shows the hamlet of Wasdale Head, with Great Gable rising majestically to the left, and the route to the Styhead Pass visible in the centre.

The hamlet of Grange in the rocky heart of Borrowdale is named after an outlying farm set up in the Middle Ages by the monks of Furness Abbey.

Another view of Borrowdale, shows the twin bridges which cross the River Derwent in the hamlet. The printed message on the back of this war-time, 1943 postcard is interesting. It quotes Winston Churchill, the Prime Minister: 'Let us all strive without failing in faith or in duty.'

The 'Jaws' or constricted entrance to Borrowdale, as seen from around Shepherd's Crag, with King's Howe prominent on the left.

One of the most famous features of Borrowdale is the Bowder Stone, seen here in the foreground with a ladder reaching to its summit. Castle Crag and Gates Crag form the backdrop.

The Bowder Stone is a 1900-ton boulder, 30 feet high, which fell away from the surrounding valley side and is now delicately perched on a narrow base inviting the brave to climb to its summit. The long-dressed Edwardian lady who has just alighted from her pony and trap in this 1912 postcard seems to be having second thoughts about it.

CASTLE CRAG, BORROWDALE, CUMBERLAND.   KW/16

Ramblers admire the view from the level summit of Castle Crag, to the south of Grange in Borrowdale. Castle Crag was recommended by Alfred Wainwright as the summit to climb if the visitor to Lakeland had only two or three hours to spare. The doyen of Lakeland guide-book writers, he claimed that the Jaws of Borrowdale were the loveliest square mile in the whole district.

Rosthwaite Valley from Castle Crag   47   Mayson

The view down to Rosthwaite village and south down the Rosthwaite Valley with Eagle Crag in the distance, from the rocky summit of Castle Crag.

The flatness of the Rosthwaite Valley in the heart of Borrowdale shows it to be the former site of a glacial lake, now drained and valuable meadowland.

Rocky crags spring up from some of the loveliest native deciduous woodlands in the Lake District in the secret heart of Borrowdale.

The minor road along the western shores of Derwent Water winds across Brandlehow on the eastern slopes of Cat Bells and then down to Manesty to enter the Jaws of Borrowdale.

Langstrath, which forms the upper, southern end of Borrowdale, has a Scottish-sounding name, and this view from Langstrath Beck looking up to Eagle Crag bears out the resemblance to landscapes north of the Border.

4008 The Vale of Newlands.

The pastoral Vale of Newlands runs parallel with Derwent Water, and contains a scatter of isolated sheep farms. This view is from the summit of Cat Bells.

The apparently-conical peak of Hindscarth stands sentinel at the end of the Newlands Valley, with the peaks of Robinson to the right and Dale Head to the left.

Wordsworth's beloved Vale of Grasmere, the tower of Grasmere church prominent in the centre, as seen looking east from above Allen Bank.

The aptly-named Bracken Fell – the fern was once harvested to provide winter bedding for livestock – and the peak of Butter Crag, as seen from Grasmere village.

1021. Grasmere and Helm Crag from Butter Crag.

We've now climbed to the rocky peak of Butter Crags, and are looking north across Grasmere village and valley towards Helm Crag in the centre of the photograph.

Longsleddale is one of the forgotten dales of the Lake District. Situated in the south-eastern corner of the district, it does not attract the crowds mainly because it does not contain a lake. But as this 1940s view of the River Sprint which drains it shows, you can still enjoy the bliss of solitude here.

Longsleddale, No. 4

Another Edwardian view of the upper end of Longsleddale, showing the rocky slopes of Cocklaw Fell which marks the dale's western side.

Deepdale Hall stands at the entrance to Deepdale, which runs south from Patterdale between St Sunday Crag and Hart Crag.

Arniston Crag, seen here in this 1932 postcard from the east, stands like a sentinel at the entrance to secluded Deepdale.

The lower slopes of St Sunday Crag (actually Gavel Pike) as seen from the confines of Deepdale.

A lovely Edwardian photographic study of the snow-streaked summit of Fairfield, as seen from Deepdale on a winter's day.

The ivy-covered packhorse bridge over St John's Beck in the Vale of St John, north of Thirlmere and east of Keswick.

Looking north towards Mellbreak and the hills and the lake in the valley of Crummock Water.

This view from the Buttermere Hotel shows the white-painted Fish Hotel to the left, and Mellbreak above Crummock Water in the background.

Looking down on Troutbeck village and valley from the slopes of Applethwaite Common, with the winding road, now the A592, climbing towards the Kirkstone Pass.

Above Boot, Eskdale, on the western side of the district, becomes much wilder and more remote with little in the way of human habitation, although this ancient arched packhorse bridge survives.

The long and winding road across Shap Fells on the eastern edge of the Lake District has long been a trial to travellers. Now virtually by-passed by the M6 motorway, the Shap Fells were notorious for high winds and blizzards in winter.

FOUR

THE PEAKS

Great Gable & Styhead from Great End   753

'I was over this Styhead Pass yesterday on a long walk and enjoyed every minute.' That's the message on the back of this Fifties postcard, which gives an aerial view of the Styhead Pass and its tarn from Great End, with Great Gable on the left.

402.
THE PILLAR AND
SCARF GAP FROM
GREAT GABLE

We are now on the summit of 2949ft. Great Gable, looking north west down Ennerdale with Pillar on the left, and a glimpse of Buttermere in the distance to the right over the Scarf Gap pass between Haystacks and High Crag.

Just seventeen years before this postcard was sent, the sport of British rock climbing was born when Walter Haskett Smith 'feeling as small as a mouse climbing a milestone' made the first ascent of Napes Needle south of the summit of Great Gable. For some unknown reason, this 1903 card is written in German.

Another view from Great Gable, this time looking from the Napes down the length of Wasdale and Lingmell Beck to Wast Water and the screes and beyond towards the Irish Sea.

This is the scene looking in the opposite direction from Great Gable. Scafell Pike, at 3210 ft the highest mountain in England, is on the extreme left of the picture, while its neighbour Scafell (3162ft) is in the centre.

A classic view of Great Gable (left), as seen from Lingmell. The route to Styhead is seen snaking across the slopes, and the Napes are just below the summit to the left.

3/50. Scawfell, Scawfell Pike and Upper Eskdale from Crinkle Crags.

Looking west towards the roof of England from Crinkle Crags, an outlier of Bowfell. Scafell (here spelt as it is said: 'Scawfell') is in the centre and Scafell Pike on the right.

In the heart of the hills looking down on Esk Hause from Great End, towards Bowfell and the south with a glimpse of Windermere in the far distance.

The last haul up to the top of Skiddaw from the slately cairn on the final part of the ascent. People can clearly be seen on the summit, which at 3054ft is the fourth highest in the Lake District, commanding a fine view across Derwent Water and Keswick.

It's Coronation Day for King George V on 23 June, 1911, and the people of Keswick have climbed to the top of their local high point of Skiddaw to mark the occasion by the building of a huge bonfire. Similar beacons were lit throughout Britain.

The ascent of Skiddaw from Keswick, a relatively easy 6-mile plod, was so popular that a hut was erected by the side of White Beck to provide refreshments for the climbers. Two crinoline-clad ladies are seen resting from their exertions on a seat outside the corrugated iron hut, while the hut keeper casts a wary eye at the weather and a young boy (left) takes notes on a slate.

The vast expanses of Skiddaw Forest stretch for many miles to the north and east of the summit of the mountain. This is little-frequented country and the path leads to one of the very few signs of man hereabouts, Skiddaw House, embowered in trees in the middle distance.

A heavily-enhanced view of the village of Threlkeld in the valley of the River Greta with the imposing escarpment of Blencathra, Skiddaw's western neighbour, in the background.

This 1909 Oilette painting shows an impossibly-romantic view of the summit of Blencathra, or Saddleback, from 'Purple Tarn.' This must be Scales Tarn, which nestles in a glacial cwm below Hallsfell Top, with Sharp Edge, an entertaining scramble, on the right.

Sharp Edge, Blencathra, is one of the most challenging approaches to any of the Lakeland hills, but should only be attempted by those skilled in rock scrambling. Combined with a return down Hallsfell Ridge, it makes a satisfying round.

Another classic ridge approach to the mountains is Striding Edge on Helvellyn, one of the most climbed mountains in Lakeland. It is seen here from Lad Crag, looking across to Red Tarn. Ullswater can just be seen across the fells of Glenridding Common.

Another view of Striding Edge on Helvellyn, this time showing the whole of the ridge to High Spying How, the sharp summit to the right.

Looking in the opposite direction to the last postcard, this view shows the northern aspect of Striding Edge from Swirral Edge, with St Sunday Crag in the background.

This is the walker's view of the approach to Striding Edge from Patterdale, and shows the 3116ft summit with Red Tarn away to the right.

Swirral Edge is the natural descent route for walkers who have ascended Helvellyn via Striding Edge. Not quite so severe, it heads towards Catstycam, the peak in the right centre, with a glimpse of Ullswater to the right. The small tarn in Brown Cove to the left is a temporary affair.

The broad expanses of High Street, which is the fell at the head of Haweswater, was once crossed by a Roman Road and later the scene of organised horse races in the nineteenth century.

A beautiful photograph of the serrated skyline of the aptly-named Crinkle Crags, which stand at the head of Oxendale, a western branch of Great Langdale.

Pillar Rock is one of the most famous natural landmarks in the Lake District. It stands to the north of the summit of Pillar mountain in Ennerdale, and was apparently first climbed by a local shepherd, John Atkinson, in 1826.

29 Stickle Tarn & Pavey Ark.

The rocky façade of Pavey Ark frowns down on the still waters of Stickle Tarn, in the heart of the Langdale Pikes. The diagonal traverse which ascends the face from bottom right to top left is known as Jack's Rake and is the climb which convinced Alfred Wainwright that he was **not** a rock climber.

THE ASCENT OF GRISDALE PIKE. 425.

The long ascent of Grisedale Pike from Braithwaite near Keswick takes the walker over Kinn and Sleet How, before the final climb to the 2593ft summit.

As described in the Northern Lakes chapter, the ascent of Cat Bells, above Derwent Water, is one of the easiest and most popular in the district.

Again we are in the heart of the hills, looking north from High Stile, the northern wall of Ennerdale, across the end of Buttermere towards Grasmoor.

Scout Scar is the limestone escarpment to the west of Kendal, which overlooks the Lyth Valley running down to the shifting sands of Morecambe Bay.

FIVE

THE PASSES

A coach and four stand outside the whitewashed walls of the Kirkstone Pass Inn, formerly known as the Traveller's Rest, a landmark on the old south-north road between Ambleside and Ullswater on the eastern side of the Lake District.

This is the Kirk Stone after which the pass takes its name, and at which dissenting Covenanters may have once held services. It stands on the descent from the summit of the Kirkstone Pass towards Brothers Water and Place Fell, seen in the distance.

960. Kirkstone Pass
and Inn from Ambleside.

An early open-topped motor car takes the long and winding minor road up the Kirkstone Pass from Ambleside, towards the distant, white-painted Kirkstone Inn on the horizon.

139."THE LAST HALF-MILE"
KIRKSTONE PASS AND INN.

Another view, amusingly-titled 'The Last Half-mile', of the ascent from Ambleside towards the Kirkstone Pass Inn.

A Morris Minor chugs up the last few yards to the summit of the Kirkstone Pass on the main A592 road, with Brothers Water and Place Fell in the background.

A hand-coloured postcard of the same scene dating from 1908. The message on the back says: 'We'll be cycling down here shortly from Windermere to Ullswater.'

KIRKSTONE PASS AND BROTHERSWATER   S.581

A view from the eastern side of the pass looking north towards Hartsop and Brothers Water – reputedly named after two brothers who drowned in its waters.

The 'New Road' across the Honister Pass, which links Borrowdale with Buttermere, as shown in a hand-coloured postcard from 1947. Honister Crag frowns down on the scene.

Another view from a similar viewpoint, which shows the road on the left winding up towards the Honister Crag quarries, which were used for the extraction of green Lakeland slate for many years.

'The Steep Bit' of the Honister Pass was obviously a severe test for these coaches-and-fours at the turn of the last century. A specially-posed Abraham photograph.

311. THE STEEP BIT. HONISTER PASS.

A close-up of 'The Steep Bit' on the old road across Honister. Note that several of the ladies have decided that discretion is the better part of valour, and are walking alongside the coaches.

At last the descent from the summit of Honister, with several people again walking down the road alongside the Gatesgarthdale Beck, which is seen on the right.

The Styhead Pass is one of the great walkers' highways of the Lake District, across some of the highest ground in England. It links Borrowdale and Wasdale via Seathwaite, Styhead Tarn and Lingmell Beck.

This Edwardian gentleman has decided to dismount from his horse on the narrowest section of the Styhead Pass.

Two more Edwardian characters take a well-earned rest on the route up the Styhead Pass, and are rewarded with a grand view down towards Seathwaite and into Borrowdale.

A fully-laden stage coach pauses for the photographer as it climbs out of Grasmere towards the summit of Dunmail Raise, now the main A591 south-north route in the district, between Grasmere and Keswick.

The motor age has arrived and the stagecoach is replaced by equally-crowded motor charabancs descending into Grasmere from Dunmail Raise. The large cairn at the summit of the Raise is said to have been erected on the site of the grave of King Dunmail of Cumbria, who died here in a tenth-century battle.

The Newlands Pass, sometimes known as Buttermere Hause, is the long minor road which winds up between Robinson and Knott Rigg from the Newlands Valley to Buttermere. This view looks north across the Sail Beck towards Knott Rigg.

A hand-coloured postcard of the same view, showing horse-drawn coaches ascending the pass.

One of the many bends on the Newlands Pass was known as 'The Devil's Elbow' and this view shows three coaches-and-fours on their way back from Buttermere to Keswick.

A slight tilting of the camera made this 1918 postcard of Buttermere Hause seem even more precarious!

The Whinlatter Pass takes the motorist between Braithewaite near Keswick and the Vale of Lorton and Cockermouth. This view looks north and shows the southern end of Bassenthwaite and the lower slopes of Skiddaw rising to the right.

Looking north down Langstrath and the Langstrath Beck from the last tree near the summit of the Stake Pass, which links Langdale with Borrowdale.

4031 Eskdale from Hardknott Pass

Perhaps the toughest test for the motorist in the Lake District are the Wrynose and Hardknott Passes, which link Little Langdale and Eskdale. This photograph is near the summit of the Hardknott, where the Romans constructed their fort of *Mediobogdum*, looking down towards the green expanses of Eskdale and the distant Irish Sea.

623 HOWTOWN, ULLSWATER AND "THE HAUSE". (ABRAHAM'S SERIES)

'Hause' is an old term for a pass, and this view shows the hairpins of Howtown Hause above the hamlet of Howtown on the eastern shores of Ullswater, which can be seen in the distance. An open-topped car struggles up the steep ascent.

SIX

THE TARNS

Perhaps one of the most famous and most photographed scenes in the entire Lake District is Tarn Hows (here in this 1913 postcard spelt 'Tarn Hawse'), tucked away in the Furness Fells between Hawkshead and Coniston. But how many of the thousands of visitors who come to admire the charming mix of trees and lakes realise that Tarn Hows is artificial – constructed in the nineteenth century by the damming of a stream?

Another view of Tarn Hows, showing the pine-topped island and a distant view of the Helvellyn range. The message on the back reads: 'After a fortnight here I shall be ready for the long promised hike over Cheviot.'

Easedale Tarn, Grasmere

21520

Easedale Tarn lies hidden away in a glacial cwm between Tarn Crag, High Raise, Sergeant Man and Blea Rigg and Crag high in the hills to the west of Grasmere. Its rocky shoreline contains many idyllic bays and beaches. This view is from the outfall of Sour Milk Gill.

After Tarn Hows, Blea Tarn is probably the most-photographed tarn in the Lakes, but this 1904 postcard gives it an overtly romantic look, with clouds dramatically wreathing the summits of the Langdale Pikes in the background.

Another view of Blea Tarn, which is tucked into the fells between Great and Little Langdale at a height of around 600 feet. The view of the distant Langdale Pikes across Great Langdale is justly famous, as the tarn and its pine trees provide the perfect foreground.

This hand-coloured postcard of Blea Tarn dates from 1904 and the writer states: 'We go wading every afternoon. We are always hungry, we are living off cream and strawberries.'

A stunning view by the Abraham brothers of Grisedale Tarn, looking down the length of Grisedale to the beckoning gleam of Ullswater in the distance. The photograph was taken from 2415 foot Seat Sandal and shows St Sunday Crag on the right with Tarn Crag on the left.

The Brothers' Parting is the name given to this inscribed rock and cairn on the eastern shores of Grisedale Tarn, where Grisedale Beck drains into Grisedale. It commemorates the parting of William Wordsworth with his brother, John, who joined the Navy in 1800 and died when HMS *Abergavenny* sank five years later. William never saw him again.

Sty Head is the great crossroads in the heart of England's highest country. This superb Abraham's postcard from 1911 shows Styhead's tarn backed by the immense bulk of Great End, the northern terminus of the Scafell range.

SEVEN

WATERFALLS

Stock Ghyll Force ('force' or 'foss' is the old Norse name for a waterfall) is among the most easily accessible of Lakeland's waterfalls, a short thirty minute walk there and back from the centre of Ambleside.

The Lower Falls at Coniston are where the waters from Levers Water and Red Dell Beck spill over a rocky outcrop, crossed by a sturdy stone bridge. The peak of the Old Man of Coniston can be seen in the background.

Just above the Dungeon Ghyll Hotel and deep in the confines of Dungeon Ghyll, which rises between Harrison Stickle and Pike of Stickle in the Langdale Pikes, are a series of spectacular waterfalls – known collectively as Dungeon Ghyll Force.

This hand-coloured postcard dating from 1906 shows the timber walkway which once wound up above the waterfalls of wild and picturesque Tilberthwaite Ghyll on the eastern slopes of Wetherlam. Most have now been swept away by the rushing waters of the ghyll.

Hilda and Lewis thought that Judith would love these ferns by the waterfalls in Stanley Ghyll, near Boot, according to the message on the back of this charming postcard which they sent her in 1941.

Scale Force, near Buttermere, is the highest single-drop waterfall in the Lake District, where Scale Beck drops a total of 172 feet in two graceful leaps down the northern slopes of Starling Dodd to enter Crummock Water. A waterfall for the connoisseur.

The 40-foot cataract of Lodore Falls, so beloved of the Romatic poets such as Robert Southey is at the south-eastern end of Derwent Water, where Watendlath Beck tumbles down between the towering wooded cliffs of Shepherd's and Gowder Crag. The falls are in the grounds of the Lodore Hotel and a small entrance charge is made for access.

Opposite and above: Perhaps the most famous and popular of the Lakeland waterfalls, Aira Force is on the western side of Ullswater, near Dockray. A short walk from the National Trust car park, the main fall, crossed by a wooden bridge in these post-cards, is 70 feet high. The wooden bridge has since been replaced by a stone one. The second view of Aira (spelt here as 'Airey') Force is a romanticised watercolour, and it is interesting to note the artistic licence employed. Aira Force was popu-larised in Wordsworth's poem *The Sonambulist*.

The Devil's Punchbowl or The Churn is the dramatic name given to this waterfall and plunge pool in Watendlath Beck, situated downstream of, and about 100 yards to the north of, the little Norse settlement of Watendlath.

Also known as Whitewater Dash, these falls 'back o' Skiddaw' were a particular favourite of Alfred Wainwright, the doyen of Lakeland fellwanderers. He thought this 65-foot cascade between Dead Crags and Little Calva deserved first place in the ranking of Lake District waterfalls. They are reached from Bassenthwaite village.

One of the many hidden gems of the Lake District, The Howk lies tucked away west of the village of Caldbeck and is unusual because the steep-sided gorge carved by the Whelpo Beck and containing the 40-foot fall is the only limestone gorge in the district.

EIGHT

TOWNS AND VILLAGES

The slate walls of Keswick's ecclesiastical-looking Moot Hall dominating the Market Square were traditionally painted white with black quoins, as seen in this 1907 hand-coloured postcard. Note the handcart left in the middle of the street, something which would certainly not be possible today.

Times have moved on, and now some of the earliest motor cars take up the space which had been occupied by the handcart, as the motor age dawns in Keswick.

A coloured photographic postcard, probably dating from the 1960s, shows the modern appearance of Keswick Market Square, with the whitewash now removed from the walls of the Moot Hall.

This 1906 postcard shows a painting of Keswick Market Square as it looked in 1867, looking down the square from near the Moot Hall. Note the horse-drawn cart on the right, which is carrying a large tree trunk.

This almost-aerial view from 1928 of Keswick and Derwent Water was taken from the slopes of Skiddaw, the smooth Ordovician slates of which rise up straight from the suburbs of the town. Cat Bells and Maiden Moor make up the background, with Borrowdale in the left distance.

An almost identical view, this time taken from a hand-coloured postcard dating from 1904. Note that in the previous picture, the large hotel in the foreground has been expanded, but the view is essentially unchanged.

A wider angle version from almost the same viewpoint which again shows the beautiful setting of the capital of northern Lakeland.

As the correspondent rightly notes in his message on the back of this 1906 postcard, the house in the trees on the left of this photograph of Greta Bridge at Keswick was where the poet Robert Southey lived. He omitted to mention that Samuel Taylor Coleridge also lived there.

The churchyard of the tiny isolated church of St John's-in-the-Vale near Keswick is famous for this splendid view, looking west towards a glimpse of Derwent Water, Catbells and and the distant Causey Pike.

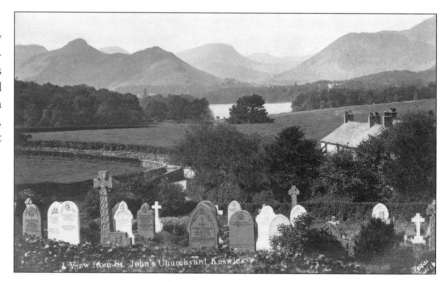

A long view of the central Lakeland town of Ambleside from Loughrigg Fell, with the spire of the fifteenth-century parish church prominent in the middle distance.

Haymaking, using a horse-drawn sledge, is in full swing on the slopes of Loughrigg Fell in this charming postcard from 1906. Note the farmworker in the centre of the photograph, who is having a well-earned swig from his basketweave bottle.

'The tree in the road' was a prominent enough feature in Church Road in Ambleside to have a postcard devoted to it in the 1960s.

A turn of the last century photograph of a long-skirted lady crossing the famous Stepping Stones over the River Rothay just outside Ambleside. No walking trousers or breeches for women then!

Another view of Ambleside's Stepping Stones, this time from a distance in a 1904 hand-coloured postcard.

The bridge over the River Rothay at Ambleside, with the peak of High Pike dominating the background.

The Old Mill at Ambleside, powered by the River Rothay. The town was once famous for its corn and bobbin mills.

The hay has been left to stand in stooks in the field adjacent to the Goldrill Beck in the tiny village of Patterdale, at the head of Ullswater. The bulk of Helvellyn fills the background.

The three-storey white-painted White Lion public house, also seen on the right of the previous post-card, is prominent in this view of Patterdale, looking north towards Glenridding Dodd.

Looking down the Goldrill Beck in Patterdale, towards Goldrill House, in a postcard which is dated 1932.

Patterdale takes its name from St Patrick, who is said to have walked here after being shipwrecked on Duddon Sands in AD 540. This view from 1933 also shows the White Lion in sunlight on the right.

On the road to Glenridding just outside the village of Patterdale facing Ullswater is this small gabled well. Legend is that this is where St Patrick stopped to drink when he arrived in Patterdale in the sixth century.

A small boy stands in the middle of the village street in Portinscale, a small village on the north-west shores of Derwent Water in this postcard, which is dated 1924.

Another view of Portinscale, this time looking in the opposite direction past the ivy-clad cottages on the left towards the white-painted Derwentwater Hotel.

The 'Auld Grey Town' of Kendal on the River Kent is the gateway to the Lake District for many visitors coming from the south. The largest town of the old county of Westmorland, Kendal was founded on the wealth won from the wool of the Lake District sheep.

Twin bridges cross the island formed in the River Derwent at Grange-in-Borrowdale, a strong candidate for one of the prettiest villages in the Lake District. Grange takes its name from being an outlying farm of the monks of Furness Abbey. This view looks towards the peak of High Spy.

1061 Chapel Stile and Langdale Pikes.

Chapel Stile is the tiny hamlet which lies at the entrance to the Langdale Valley, and the famous pikes of Harrison and Pike of Stickle can be seen peeping over the shoulder of Thrang Crag on the right.

A Misty Morning.
Newby Bridge,
Windermere.

The sixteenth-century five-arched bridge spanning the River Leven as it makes its way from Windermere to Morecambe Bay gave its name to the village of Newby Bridge. This charming water-colour postcard shows a pair of swans making their way under the bridge as two children watch on.

An early four-view postcard from Windermere, showing the lake and town on England's largest freshwater lake. The coat of arms features the char fish found in the lake, and the picture in the bottom right hand corner is interesting, because it shows two stage coaches on the steam-powered cross-lake ferry near Bowness.

A 1903 view of Bowness on Windermere, showing an oarsman on the lake in the foreground, obligingly posing for the camera. The scene is much busier with pleasure boats today.

A far busier scene at Bowness, with a flotilla of rowing boats moored on the landing waiting for their customers to take them out on the lake.

A new-fangled motor car chugs down the 'new' Promenade at Bowness, while a family watch the photographer suspiciously on the right. The Promenade Gardens followed the coming of the railway to Bowness in 1847. In the background can be seen the tower of St Martin's parish church.

The small oval tarn at the northern end of Esthwaite Water and south of Hawkshead, seen here in the background, is known as Priest's Pot. St Michael's church at Hawkshead, reflected in the tarn, is one of the most interesting and most substantial in the Lake District, dating from the fifteenth century.

A similar view of Hawkshead across Priest's Pot with the bulk of Wetherlam filling the background, from a hand-coloured postcard dating from 1904.

The Main Street, Hawkshead, looking towards the Market Square. Hawkshead retains its narrow, medieval streets, which are now thankfully bypassed by most traffic. Note the old-fashioned AA sign on the left.

The Pelter Bridge spans the River Rothay in Wordsworth's Rydal, beneath the rocky slopes of Loughrigg Fell. A coloured postcard from 1906.

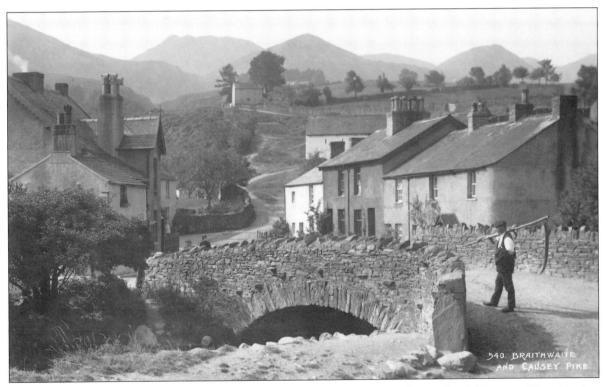

A farm worker shoulders his scythe at the end of another hard day cutting hay in the fields around Braithwaite, a small hamlet 2 miles west of Keswick where the Coledale Beck joins the Newlands Beck. Causey Pike is in the background.

Another view of Braithwaite, with a glimpse of Bassenthwaite Lake in the right distance, and the slopes of Braithwaite Fell and Lord's Seat forming the backdrop.

The former mining hamlet of Boot lies midway along Eskdale in the central fells. This Fifties postcard shows the narrow, hump-back bridge in the centre of the hamlet, which is a popular stop on the narrow-guage Ravenglass and Eskdale light railway.

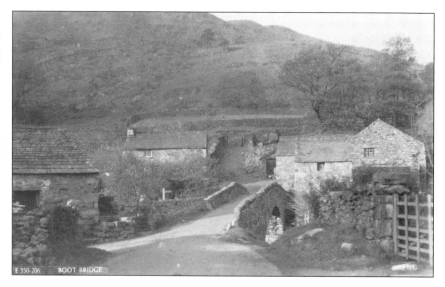

The stone-built gabled porch, seen here in the Borrowdale hamlet of Stonethwaite, is a common feature of traditional vernacular architecture in Lakeland. The prominent crag in the background is Heron Crag, a popular place for rock climbers.

A Lakeland Character, Vivian Fisher, Keswick. 5.541.

Described here as 'A Lakeland Character', Vivian Fisher of Keswick was a well-known sight to visitors during the Sixties on the narrow road which climbs up from Derwent Water to the tiny hamlet of Watendlath. He installed this gate across the public road, and would open it obligingly for passing motorists, wishing them a cheery 'Good morning.' The basket was soon filling with donations.

Footpath erosion is nothing new if this 1922 postcard showing the well-worn and popular footpath which leads up from the Norse hamlet of Watendlath to Rosthwaite is to be believed. Watendlath, which stands by its own tarn, featured in Hugh Walpole's novel *Judith Paris*.

The packhorse bridge at Watendlath leads up to the footpath to Rosthwaite in Borrowdale mentioned in the previous caption. Watendlath hamlet is now in the care of the National Trust.

Looking south from Pooley Bridge, the village on the River Eamont which stands at the northern end of Ullswater, with a distant glimpse of the lake. This Abraham photograph dates from the turn of the last century and shows another blissfully traffic-free scene.

Visitors are enjoying the sun on the sweeping concrete seawall at Silloth, the small seaside town on the Solway Firth on the northern edge of the Lake District.

Another view of Silloth, this time showing the Green with the spire of the parish church of Christ Church in the background. Donkey rides appear to be being provided on the green to the right of the photograph.

Seascale, on the western coastline of Lakeland, is usually associated with the Sellafield Nuclear Power Station just to the north of the village, which is now one of the top wet-weather visitor attractions in the Lake District. This photograph shows the headland of The Neb.

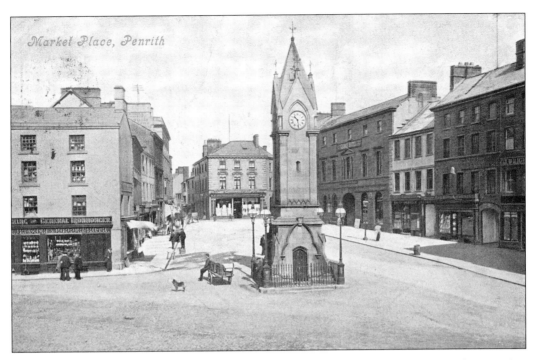

Penrith, the small town which prides itself as the capital of the north-eastern Lake District, received its market charter as long ago as 1223, and has been a busy market town ever since. This view from 1904 shows the Clock Tower and a deserted Market Place.

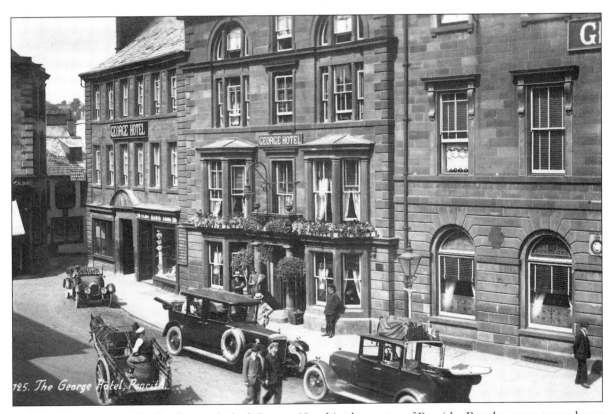

A far busier scene outside the flower-decked George Hotel in the centre of Penrith. But the open-topped cars parked outside the hotel have not yet superseded real horse power, as the horse and cart on the left indicate.

The dog roses are in full bloom in the foreground of this distant shot of the village of Ireby, which lies in the valley of the River Ellen to the north of Skiddaw and Bassenthwaite Lake.

Allonby is a small, linear village lying on the Solway Firth between Maryport and Silloth. It has the distinction of having the broad bay on the firth on which it stands being named after it.

Wigton, birthplace of Lord Melvyn Bragg, is a pleasant market town on the broad Solway Plain, with much good Georgian architecture as shown here. Hetherington, the name on the shop front (centre) is another common local name.

NINE

CHURCHES AND CASTLES

A fully-loaded coach–and–four stands outside the tiny whitewashed church at Wythburn, a typical Lake District church with a small bell cote on the west gable end, and an extended chancel on the east. The slopes of Helvellyn rise behind.

St Patrick's church in Patterdale, with its detached tower, is famous for its tapestries by Ann Macbeth, a former resident of the village. The message on the back of the postcard describes how 'two nice boys' had taken Margaret and her friend climbing 'and we got lost in a mountain mist, and were lucky to get to the hostel.'

'M.A.' writes on this postcard that 'This is the church where I go twice every Sunday. It is a very pretty church.' Bowness-on-Solway is notable chiefly for being the westernmost extremity of Hadrian's Wall and boasts a Roman fort facing the Dumfries hills in Scotland, across the Solway Firth.

The bulk of Hallin Fell fills the background of this post-card of St Peter's church, Martindale, another typical Lakeland church with bell cote at the western end. Martindale is a small village south of Howtown in the fells on the eastern side of Ullswater, and despite being in one of the smallest parishes in the country, it boasts two churches, St Peter's and St Martin's.

Crosthwaite church, just outside Keswick, has an unusual dedication to St Kentigern (the Scottish St Mungo of Glasgow). Built in the Perpendicular style, it is one of the oldest and most interesting churches in the Lake District, and contains the tomb of Robert Southey with an inscription by Wordsworth, and some lovely stained glass.

Above and below: The tiny chapel that is Buttermere church stands high above the village between the lakes of Buttermere and Crummock Water, which is glimpsed in the background of this sepia postcard. It lays a good claim to being the most beautifully-situated Lakeland church with outstanding views all around, here looking across towards Mellbreak. The interior of the church is very plain and simple, like so many others of its kind in Lakeland.

Above and below: St Oswald's church, Grasmere, seen here reflected in the waters of the River Rothay, is perhaps best-known as the last resting place of poet William Wordsworth, his wife and sister. He accurately describes the thirteenth-century church in *The Excursion* as a building of 'rude and antique majesty,' and the interior, seen in the next postcard, with 'pillars crowded' and 'naked rafters intricately crossed.'

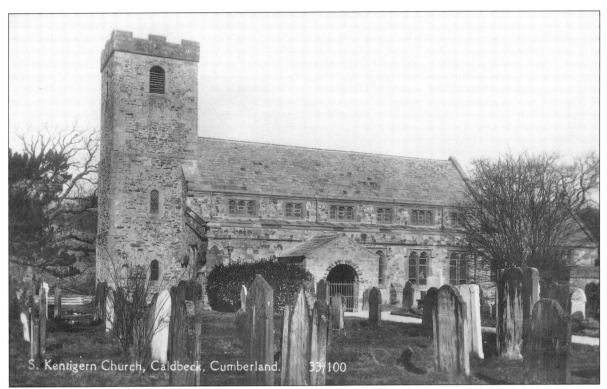

S. Kentigern Church, Caldbeck, Cumberland.   33/100

We met the Celtic Saint Kentigern earlier at Crosthwaite, and he appears again here as the patron saint of Caldbeck parish church, on the northern boundary of the Lake District. Perhaps the most famous occupant of the churchyard is the renowned huntsman, John Peel, who was born at Caldbeck in 1776 and buried here in 1854 after being killed in a hunting accident.

NEWLANDS PARISH CHURCH. NO. 4.

The Newlands valley, west of Derwent Water, is one of few in the Lake District where the scars of industry can be seen. Copper and lead were mined here from Tudor times, and even the Victorian parish church seen here, was surrounded by forestry plantations.

Lorton stands in the fertile valley between Crummock Water and Cockermouth, and is divided into Low and High Lorton. The sturdy parish church with its pinnacled tower seen here is in Low Lorton, in the valley of the River Cocker.

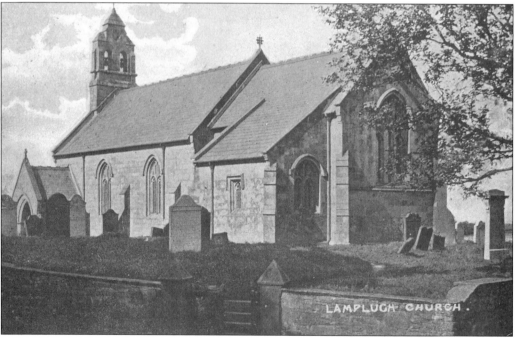

The parish church of St Michael at Lamplugh between Loweswater and Ennerdale in the north west of the district, is noted for its double bell cote, seen here at the western end of the church, which was restored in 1870.

RUINS OF LANERCOST ABBEY. BRAMPTON.

The red sandstone ruins of Lanercost Priory stand above the River Irthing near Brampton. The priory was founded in 1166 by Augustinian monks, and the nave now forms the parish church of St Mary Magdalene for the village.

S 4646, Interior, Parish Church, Penrith.

This postcard of the interior of St Andrew's parish church at Penrith shows the formal Georgian architecture of the nave. This part of the church was rebuilt in the eighteenth century possibly to the design of Nicholas Hawksmoor, a pupil of Christopher Wren. The squat tower, however, dates from the thirteenth and fourteenth centuries.

Mirrored in the waters of the River Eamont, the ruined towers of Brougham Castle stand 2 miles south-east of Penrith. The red sandstone castle was originally built in Norman times, and was the last home of the legendary Lady Anne Clifford.

855. The Castle. Kendal.
(Abrahams' Series)

Kendal Castle, the guant ruins of which now stand in a public park near the town centre, was the birthplace of Katherine Parr, the last wife of Henry VIII. At the time, the originally thirteenth-century castle was in the hands of her father, Sir Thomas Parr.

A herd of fallow deer make the perfect foreground to this postcard of Lowther Castle, near Penrith, on the north-eastern boundary of the district. The 'castle' was built in castellated, Gothic style by Robert Smirke for the first Earl of Lonsdale in 1806-11. It is now a wildlife park and adventure playground.

Appleby Castle dominates the former Westmorland town on the River Eden, which is famous for its Gypsy and Horse Fair held in June. This view from the twelfth-century keep looks across the ivy-clad courtyard of the castle, which was restored by Lady Anne Clifford in 1653.

TEN

BUILDINGS AND MONUMENTS

A heavily-enhanced colour postcard from 1904 of the so-called 'Druid's Circle' near Keswick, with Saddleback, now usually known as Blencathra, in the background. The Castlerigg stone circle dates from the Neolithic or early Bronze Age periods, and has nothing whatever to do with Druids.

Another, later, view of the Castlerigg circle with some visitors on the left of the photograph struggling with a map in the high winds which often sweep across the monument.

1041. Lyulph's Tower, Ullswater.

According to the message on the back of this 1931 postcard of Lyulph's Tower, near Aira Force on the shores of Ullswater: 'The ivy is all off now – the three windows upstairs this side are the sitting room and staircase.' The name of the tower is thought to come from 'Ulf', a former Baron of Greystoke, after whom Ullswater is said to take its name.

The Dam, Haweswater.

Water spills spectacularly over the dam wall which impounds Haweswater, in the eastern Lake District. The dam was built in 1934 to flood the valley and scattered village of Mardale and provide Manchester with supplies of clean, fresh Lakeland water. The dam is 96 feet high and 1550 feet long and it impounds about 18,600 million gallons of water.

Penrith, Mardale, Dun Bull Hotel.

The Dun Bull Hotel, standing under Harter Fell at the head of Mardale, was one of the buildings which had to be sacrificed in the interests of providing far-off Manchester with water. The ruins of the substantial building – described in Baddeley's *Thorough Guide* of 1909 as 'a capital little hostelry' – are still revealed at times of severe drought, such as happened in 1984.

A wintry scene revealing Patterdale Hall in a setting more like Canada than Cumberland. Patterdale Hall stands in its wooded surrounds at the southern end of Ullswater, above the village of the same name.

Wastwater Hotel.

The Wastwater Hotel, seen here in a 1941 postcard, was the birthplace of British rock climbing, and early exponents such as O.G. Jones, the Abraham brothers of Keswick, and W.P. Haskett Smith often stayed here. The hotel is situated at the head of Wasdale and surrounded by the highest summits in England.

A pinafore-clad servant girl stands on the landing outside the Angler's Inn on Ennerdale Lake in this postcard from 1912. The Angler's Inn is one of the best-known hostelries in the Lake District.

PRINCE OF WALES HOTEL, GRASMERE.

A hand-coloured postcard of the grand Prince of Wales Hotel in Grasmere, with Helm Crag peeping over the chimney pots in the background. Note the horse-drawn cabs on the roadway and the absence of any other traffic on the road.

Rowing boats are drawn up on the lakeside in this sepia-toned postcard of the Waterhead Hotel at Waterhead, Ambleside, on the northernmost extremity of Windermere.

Another of Lakeland's grandest hotels in the Keswick Hotel which stands at the foot of Skiddaw and overlooks the town's Fitz Park, as seen in this postcard from 1913. The message on the back of the card says: 'I think this is the loveliest place ever I have been at, we are going to climb Skiddaw tomorrow if it is fine.'

A pair of vintage motor cars stand outside 'Ye Pheasant Hotel' at Bassenthwaite Lake in this vintage postcard. The Pheasant Inn is still providing accommodation and sustenance to visitors beneath Wythop Woods at the northern end of the lake.

OWE, Patterdale.
Copyright.

4024. ULLSWATER HOTEL.

Rhododendrons form a colourful foreground to this photograph of the grand façade of the Ullswater Hotel, on the shores of the lake of the same name.

The Fish Hotel at Buttermere hit the national headlines in 1802 when Mary Robinson, the daughter of the landlord and known as 'The Beauty of Buttermere' married a 'gentleman' who turned out to be a fraudster by the name of John Hatfield. He was later tried and hanged at Carlisle.

The other hotel at Buttermere is known as The Bridge, and this postcard shows its beautiful setting in the low ground between Buttermere and Crummock Water. The view looks west towards the conifers of Burtness Wood and the slopes of High Stile.

The fortress-like house known as Hassness lies midway along the eastern shore of Buttermere beneath the impending wall of Goat Crag, a playground for rock climbers, in the background.

The Swan at Thornthwaite is another well-known Lake District hostelry, overlooking Bassenthwaite Lake, seen here in the middle distance with the plantation-cloaked slopes of Dodd Wood and the summit of Skiddaw in the background.

The flag is flying outside the Borrowdale Hotel, in Borrowdale, near Keswick in this postcard. Note the open-topped motor car in the centre of the photograph and the slate walls of the hotel.

Stybarrow Dodd ('Crag' in the caption) forms the backdrop to this charming Edwardian scene in the gardens of Milcrest's Hotel at Glenridding, on the shores of Ullswater.

ELEVEN

YOUTH HOSTELS

Many peoples' (including the writer's) introduction to the Lake District was on school trips, staying at youth hostels. This remote, white-washed hostel at Hollows, below High Spy no longer exists and the hostel in Borrowdale is now at Longthwaite.

3127. Thorney How Youth Hostel, Grasmere.

Thorney How Youth Hostel at Grasmere is still there, and has the distinction of being the first hostel bought by the Youth Hostels Association, in 1931, just a year after the foundation of the association.

The familiar green triangle adorns the white gate at the entrance to Thorney How, which was originally a farmhouse. Despite more recent extensions and modernisation, it retains its rural character and now sleeps 53 people.

A favourite hostel for the exploration of the Langdale fells, High Close at Loughrigg, near Ambleside is officially described as a rambling Victorian mansion with open fires. Owned by the National Trust, it stands in its own extensive grounds between Elterwater and Grasmere.

Now known as Borrowdale Youth Hostel, Longthwaite is set in the heart of the Borrowdale hills at the southern end of Derwentwater. With 88 beds, this is now a three-star hostel, much upgraded since this postcard was produced.

The Buttermere Youth Hostel was formerly known as the King George VI Memorial Hostel, and stands about half a mile south of Buttermere village on the road towards the Honister Pass and Borrowdale. It is now a three-star, 70-bed hostel.

This is one hostel that it is still best to walk to. Coniston Coppermines is about a mile and a quarter from Coniston village, up a rough, unsurfaced track, and is in a converted copper mine worker's house. Note the triangular slate chimney pots.

TWELVE

LITERARY LANDMARKS

William Wordsworth, England's best-known Romantic poet, was born in this Georgian town house in Cockermouth's Main Street in 1770. His father was steward to Sir James Lowther, and the family moved here in 1766. The house overlooks the River Derwent and has a delightful garden and terrace, recently restored and in the care of the National Trust.

This is the typical Lake District cottage in Hawkshead where William Wordsworth lodged with Dame Tyson while he attended the local Grammar School from 1779 to 1787. Note the slate-built barn to the left and the staircase leading up to it.

Another view of Wordsworth's lodgings in Hawkshead, showing the outside stone staircase leading to the upper floor.

Wordsworth lived with his beloved sister Dorothy at Dove Cottage, just outside Grasmere, from 1799 to 1813, and he wrote some of his best-known poetry here. The cottage now forms part of a museum run by the National Trust and dedicated to the life and work of the poet.

Another view of Dove Cottage, seen from the lane leading up from the village at the junction of what is now the busy A591.

The library inside Dove Cottage, showing a bust of Wordsworth by the fireplace, and various portraits of him and his fellow Romantics on the walls.

Rhododendron-fringed Rydal Mount was the final home of William Wordsworth from 1813 until his death in 1850. The peaceful, reed-fringed shores of Rydal Water made it one of his favourite lakes. It is now in the hands of the National Trust.

The array of Wordsworth graves in Grasmere churchyard. The central tombstone marks the graves of the poet William, who died in 1850, and his wife, Mary. William's brother, John lies to the left, and next is William's talented sister and life-long companion, Dorothy. At the extreme left are William and Fanny, his son and daughter-in-law, while on the right are buried Edward and Dora Quillinan, William's daughter and son-in-law.

John Ruskin, one of Britain's greatest writers and social reformers, lived at Brantwood on the eastern shore of Coniston Water between 1872 and his death in 1900, latterly suffering from lengthy bouts of depression.

This view of Brantwood is taken from Coniston Water, and shows the sylvan setting of Ruskin's home. Ruskin bought Brantwood without actually seeing it in 1871, and later described the view from it as 'the finest I know in Cumberland and Lancashire – with the sunset visible over the same.'

This photograph of Ruskin was taken towards the end of his long life in the grounds of his beloved Brantwood, where he loved to roam and admire the views across the lake to Coniston Old Man.

The Celtic cross made from the olive green Coniston slate which marks Ruskin's grave in Coniston churchyard. Ruskin had expressed his wish to be buried here, rather than have a grander tomb in Westminster Abbey.

Hill Top, Sawrey was the home between 1905 and 1943 of Beatrix Potter, the creator of the evergreen childrens' favourites Peter Rabbit, Mrs Tiggywinkle and Jemima Puddleduck. Later in life, Beatrix married a local solicitor and became a well-known breeder of Herdwick sheep. The house, the most popular visitor attraction in the Lake District, is now in the care of the National Trust.

Fold Head Farm in the tiny Norse settlement of Watendlath, high in the fells above Derwent Water, is the alleged home of Judith Paris, heroine of the novel of the same name. *Judith Paris* was written by Sir Hugh Walpole, who lived on the shores of Derwent Water between 1932 and 1941.

This is Brackenburn, the slate-walled home of Sir Hugh Walpole, author of *The Herries Chronicles* and *Judith Paris*, on the shores of Derwent Water, near Keswick.

The poet Robert Southey followed his brother-in-law, Samuel Taylor Coleridge, to live in some style at Greta Hall, Keswick, in 1803. He became Poet Laureate in 1813.